MW00915915

My goal is to

Entertain ■ Educate ■ Empower

children by telling meaningful Stories
while teaching Sign Language!

Mr.C

Company is Coming!
Cleaning My Room Story
ASL - American Sign Language Book for Kids and Beginners
Stories and Signs with Mr.C - Book 7

Story Written by Mr.C - Randall Clarkson

Design & Illustrations by Deonna Clarkson

© 2016 by RDCmedia—Randall & Deonna Clarkson

StoriesAndSigns.com

Positive Repetition

is a learning method that rewards your child in a positive way.

- **Read through the story in one sitting**. Note that the words printed in color correspond with the characters in the pictures above.

- **Go back to the beginning of the book and begin to sign**. Your child will see the signs as an actual part of the story which is now familiar to them.

- **Parents can sign the two signs** shown on each page and have your child copy you. Try not to touch their hands as they first struggle to find the sign themselves. They are exploring how they can manipulate on their own.

- **Note the <u>underlined words</u>**. These are the sign language words which were read and signed earlier in the story.

- **Continue to re-read each book** until all the signs listed in the back are learned. Your child will love re-reading the books and the feeling of mastering the signs more and more.

- **Use these new sign language words** throughout the day, reinforcing them to memory.

The **Positive Repetition** of the sign language words will

engage the memory, entertain the heart & **empower your child**.

Thank you for giving your child the gift of Sign Language!

Company is Coming!

BOOK 7 of the **Stories and Signs** Series

by

Mr.C

Randall Clarkson

"At the end of this book,
I have two special gifts just for you!
Be sure and use your hands to
learn the sign words!"

Mr.C

swim

Flat hands by chest - push forward and out like you're swimming

eat

With fingers bunched together - move your hand to and from mouth a couple times

Drew was swimming in a great big bowl of spaghetti.

WHAT?!

He could eat the meatballs as he floated past on his back. The noodles were soft and tickled him.

WHAT?!

It was fun to eat and swim at the same time!

yes

Make an "S" fist
Shake it back & forward like
nodding your head

no

Pointer and tall finger on top -
thumb on the bottom - snap
them together

RING! RING! RING!

The sound of the phone woke Drew from such a wonderful dream.

He shot out of bed and ran into the kitchen as he heard his Mom say, "Yes…Yes…No…Yes…No… OK, goodbye."

What could all those yes' and no's mean?

who ?

Bend and unbend the pointer
finger of the "L" hand with the
thumb tip touching chin

what ?

Open hands palms up - shake
them back and forth and look
like you're asking a question

"Who was on the phone, Mom?" asked Drew in between bites of his breakfast.

"That was someone very special. We have guests coming over to our house today," said Mom.

"What? Guests?" Drew slowed his eating. "Who?"

"You'll be surprised!" she said with a grin.

where

Move your pointer finger back and forth a few times

when

One pointer finger makes a circle around the other pointer finger and then lands on it

Drew put his spoon down and asked, "Where are they now and when will they be here?"

"They are on their way right now. They should be here any minute," said Mom.

Drew yelled as he jumped down from his chair and ran back to his bedroom. He slammed the door behind him and looked around his room.

clean

One hand—palm up
Other hand—brush your flat
hand two times

why

Open hand touches head -
pulls away from head and
makes a "Y" hand

It was a mess...a BIG mess...and special guests are coming over any minute!"

"Mo..." Drew started to yell to his Mom but he stopped when he remembered what she always told him...'You made the mess, you clean it up!'

Drew knew that he had disobeyed his Mom the night before and that's why he should clean the room himself.

wash

Put one fist on top of the
other with fingers together -
rub them in a circle

room

Pretend to touch both sides
and front/back of a
square room

Drew's Mom works hard at her office and <u>when</u> she gets home she cooks, washes our dishes and clothes and <u>cleans</u> every room in the house.

She <u>cleans</u> and washes even though *she* didn't make the mess.

If Drew would have obeyed his Mom last night, his room would have looked alright this morning.

Have *you* ever forgotten to <u>clean</u> your <u>room</u>?

clothes

Palms against chest - brush down your shirt two times

play

Make two fists with pinkies and thumbs sticking out - turn and shake back and forth

Drew's Mom had <u>washed</u> all of his dirty clothes and, <u>when</u> she took them out of the drier, she folded them and put them on Drew's bed.

"Put your clothes <u>where</u> they belong" she had said.

Runnn! Bang! Crash! Screech!

"OK, Mom," said Drew as he kept playing with his toys.

time

Point to wrist of other hand
where a watch would be

bed

Hands together - put by right
ear and lay your head on it
like a pillow

Later, <u>when</u> it was time for Drew to go to bed, he was grumpy and tired.

"Get off of my bed, <u>clothes</u>!" and he picked up the folded <u>clothes</u> and threw them up into the air!

Was *that* the right thing to do?

Now...his <u>clothes</u> were on top of everything and time was running out before the guests would be here.

shelf

Put flat fingers together -
move them outward in a
straight line

book

Put both flat hands together -
open them up keeping
pinkies together

There were <u>clothes</u> on his shelves.

There were <u>clothes</u> on his computer.

There were <u>clothes</u> on his books.

There were <u>clothes</u> on his games.

There were <u>clothes</u> on his <u>bed</u> and even <u>clothes</u> on his dog!

<u>WHAT</u> A MESS!!

Can *you* help Drew put away his <u>clothes</u>?

socks

Two pointer fingers point
downward taking turns up
and down

underwear

Thumbs and pointer fingers
start in the middle and then
pull them outward

<u>What</u> should he do with his socks?

Can he put red and white ones together? Should he put his socks on the <u>shelves</u>?

<u>No</u>! <u>Where</u> should he put his socks?

<u>What</u> should he do with his underwear? Should he put his underwear under his <u>bed</u>?

<u>No</u>! <u>Where</u> should he put his underwear?

pants

Pull upward with both hands
like pulling up your pants

t-shirt

Make a "T" with your two
pointer fingers - then pinch
and pull your shirt

<u>What</u> should Drew do with his pants? Should he put his pants on his <u>books</u>? <u>No</u>!

<u>Where</u> should he put his pants?

<u>What</u> should he do with his t-shirts? Scrunch them up and throw them in his closet?

<u>No</u>!

<u>Where</u> should he put his t-shirts?

Do *you* ever help put away *your* <u>clothes</u>?

coat

Both fists at the top of your shoulders - pull them down like putting a coat on

shoes

Make two "S" fists and bump them together two times

<u>What</u> should Drew do with his coat? Shove it under his pillow? <u>No</u>!

<u>Where</u> should he put his coat?

<u>What</u> about his shoes? Should he just throw them under his <u>bed</u>? <u>No</u>!

<u>Where</u> should he put his shoes?

It's not easy <u>cleaning</u> up a messy <u>room</u>. Do *you* think Drew can <u>clean</u> it by himself?

table

Both arms horizontal - top
arm taps on bottom arm twice

floor

Hands side by side in front of
you - pull apart quickly

Good job Drew...all the clothes are put away!

Now, what should Drew do with all of his books that are piled on the table and floor?

Where do you keep your books?

OK...they are all off the floor and table and now they're back on the shelves.

His room is starting to look better...does he have time to play a little bit?

game

Make two fists - bump
together pinkie fingers twice

box

Pretend to touch both sides
and front/back of
a square box

No time to play now...there are still a couple things left to clean up.

Drew had been playing with several games and the pieces are not in their boxes.

Should he scoop them all up together and throw them into the toy box? Or should he first put the pieces into their own game box?

What do *you* think he should do? Why?

mess

Make your hands look like
they're holding a ball - turn
them back + forth / icky face

stop

Flat hand palm up - other
hand flat - let it fall with little
finger hitting flat hand below

The <u>games</u> are put away in each <u>box</u> and there is only one thing left to fix...his messy <u>bed</u>.

"Mo...," Drew started to yell but he stopped himself.

"Wait a second...<u>*who*</u> messed up my <u>bed</u>? Maybe I'm not big enough to make my <u>bed</u> all by myself."

Then he stopped and remembered what his teacher told him...

Point to your chest
with your pointer
finger

I

will

Hold open hand up
by ear - let it drop
forward

try!

Brush thumbs
against chest -
move fists outward

pillow

1. Hold fingers up - squeeze
2. Lay head on palm of hand

bear

Cross arms across chest and
wiggle claw fingers

Drew tried to throw the blankets up in the air like his Mom does but they never landed straight. Did Drew give up? _No_ *way!*

He ran around and around the <u>bed</u> until each side was pretty straight. He put his pillow at one end and he had his teddy bears all lined up, except one special bear.

He put *that* bear facing down like it was taking a nap on his pillow. He thought that was funny!

Grandpa

Open palm hand - touch
thumb on forehead - move
out in two small arches

Grandma

Make a "5" with your hand
Put thumb on chin - move out
in two small arches

'Ding Dong!' the front bell rang.

"Mom, someone is at the door!" said Drew as he <u>ran</u> out of his <u>bedroom</u>.

"Go ahead and open it, it must be our special guests!" said Mom.

"Grandpa, Grandma!" squealed Drew as he gave them tackle football hugs.

"Come with me!" said Drew as he pulled them down the hallway.

Mom

Make a "5" hand and put your thumb on your chin

Dad

Make a "5" with your hand - touch thumb to forehead

Drew stepped into his <u>room</u> and said, "Tada!"

"Wow," said <u>Grandpa</u>, "Did your Mom help you <u>clean</u> your <u>room</u>?"

"<u>No</u>."

"Did your Dad help you <u>clean</u> your <u>room</u>?"

"<u>No</u>."

"Did your dog..."

"<u>No</u>! I <u>cleaned</u> my <u>room</u> all by myself!"

run

Hook pointer finger to thumb
of other hand - move them
forward - pointer fingers
bending in and out

smile

Two pointer fingers draw a
smile on your face starting on
your chin upward

Drew's <u>Mom</u> came running down the hall, "<u>What</u>'s going on? <u>Why</u> are you standing in Drew's doorway smiling?"

Then her eyes went wide. She couldn't believe what she was seeing!

"Did *you* <u>clean</u> your own <u>room</u> and make your own <u>bed</u>?" she asked.

"I sure did!" said Drew with a great big smile.

proud

Make a fist and pull thumb
up your chest

more

Bunch fingers on both hands -
bump together 2-3 times

Everyone said how proud they were of Drew *but* no one was more proud than Drew was of himself. Once more Drew proudly said...

"I don't say I can't... I say I will try!"

How do *you* feel <u>when</u> you pick up your toys and <u>clean</u> your <u>bedroom</u>?

I hope it makes you <u>smile</u>!

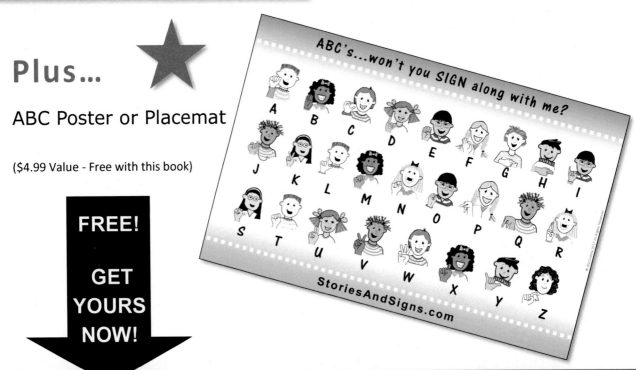

More **Stories and Signs** with Mr.C

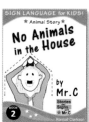

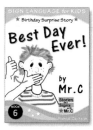

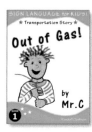

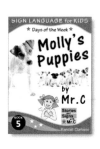

★ **The ABC's** — ASL Alphabet Signs

#1 **Out of Gas!** — Transportation Story

#2 **No Animals in the House** — Animals Story

#3 **The Big Sandwich** — Fun Foods Story

#4 **Rainy Day Play** — Indoor & Outdoor Play

#5 **Molly's Puppies** — Days of the Week

#6 **Best Day Ever!** — Birthday Surprise

#7 **Company is Coming!** — Cleaning My Room

#8 **Haunted Baseball Park** — Being Brave & Smart

Can you Sign these words from the Story?

(mess)

* swim
* eat
* yes
* no
* who
* what
* where
* when
* clean
* why
* wash
* bedroom
* clothes
* play

* bed
* time
* shelves
* book
* socks
* underwear
* pants
* t-shirt
* coat
* shoes
* table
* floor
* game
* box

* pillow
* stop
* mess
* bear
* Grandpa
* Grandma
* Mom
* Dad
* run
* smile
* proud
* more

We would like to dedicate this book to
our five amazing Grandchildren...

Meadow ♥ Logan ♥ Dani ♥ Austin ♥ Drew

...and the thousands of kids who
have learned sign language words
while laughing & enjoying our stories.

Mr.C   AUTHOR/TEACHER/PAPA
Mrs.C   ILLUSTRATOR/GRAMA

Made in the USA
Monee, IL
26 August 2022